WARS THAT CHANGED AMERICAN HISTORY

The Korean War

Robin Doak

WORLD ALMANAC® LIBRARY

Please visit our Web site at: www.garethstevens.com
For a free color catalog describing World Almanac® Library's list of high-quality books
and multimedia programs, call 1-800-848-2928 (USA) or 1-800-387-3178 (Canada).
World Almanac® Library's fax: (414) 332-3567

Library of Congress Catalog-in-Publication Data

Doak, Robin S. (Robin Santos), 1963-
  The Korean War / by Robin Doak. — North American ed.
    p. cm. — (Wars that changed American history)
  Includes bibliographical references and index.
  ISBN-10: 0-8368-7294-0 – ISBN-13: 978-0-8368-7294-1 (lib. bdg.)
  ISBN-10: 0-8368-7303-3 – ISBN-13: 978-0-8368-7303-0 (softcover)
  1. Korean War, 1950-1953—Juvenile literature. 2. Korean War, 1950-1953
—United States—Juvenile literature. I. Title. II. Series.
  DS918.D63   2006
  951.904'2—dc22   2006011595

First published in 2007 by
World Almanac® Library
A Member of the WRC Media Family of Companies
330 West Olive Street, Suite 100
Milwaukee, WI 53212 USA

Copyright © 2007 by World Almanac® Library.

A Creative Media Applications, Inc. Production
Design and Production: Alan Barnett, Inc.
Editor: Susan Madoff
Copy Editor: Laurie Lieb
Proofreader: Laurie Lieb and Donna Drybread
Indexer: Nara Wood
World Almanac® Library editorial direction: Mark J. Sachner
World Almanac® Library editor: Alan Wachtel
World Almanac® Library art direction: Tammy West
World Almanac® Library production: Jessica Morris

Picture credits: Associated Press: pages 5, 8, 9, 10, 12, 13, 14, 15, 17, 20, 21, 23, 24, 26, 30, 32, 34, 36, 38, 41, 43;
The Library of Congress: pages 28; maps courtesy of Ortelius Design

Printed in the United States of America

1 2 3 4 5 6 7 8 9 10 09 08 07 06

Table of Contents

Cover: U.S. soldiers supported by a tank division move out for an assault on an enemy-held hill in South Korea in February 1951. Smoke from tank fire on suspected enemy hideouts is seen in the background of the photograph.

3

INTRODUCTION

From the time when America declared its independence in the 1700s to the present, every war in which Americans have fought has been a turning point in the nation's history. All of the major wars of American history have been bloody, and all of them have brought tragic loss of life. Some of them have been credited with great results, while others partly or entirely failed to achieve their goals. Some of them were widely supported; others were controversial and exposed deep divisions within the American people. None will ever be forgotten.

The American Revolution created a new type of nation based on the idea that the government should serve the people. As a result of the Mexican-American War, the young country expanded dramatically. Controversy over slavery in the new territory stoked the broader controversy between Northern and Southern states over the slavery issue and powers of state governments versus the federal government. When the slave states seceded, President Abraham Lincoln led the Union into a war against the Confederacy—the Civil War—that reunited a divided nation and ended slavery.

▼ *Wars have shaped the history of the United States of America since the nation was founded in 1776. Conflict in this millennium continues to alter the decisions the government makes and the role the United States plays on the world stage.*

Wars That Changed America

							2001–
		1846–1848		**1914–1918**	**1950–1953**		Conflicts in Iraq
		Mexican-American War		World War I	Korean War		and Afghanistan
1750	1800	1850	1900		1950		2000
	1775–1783		**1861–1865**		**1939–1945**	**1964–1975**	
	American Revolution		Civil War		World War II	Vietnam War	

The roles that the United States played in World War I and World War II helped transform the country into a major world power. In both these wars, the entry of the United States helped turn the tide of the war.

Later in the twentieth century, the United States engaged in a Cold War rivalry with the Soviet Union. During this time, the United States fought two wars to prevent the spread of communism. The Korean War essentially ended in a stalemate, and after years of combat in the Vietnam War, the United States withdrew. Both claimed great numbers of American lives, and following its defeat in Vietnam, the United States became more cautious in its use of military force.

That trend changed when the United States led the war that drove invading Iraqi forces from Kuwait in 1990. After the al-Qaeda terrorist attacks of September 11, 2001, the United States again led a war, this time against Afghanistan, which was sheltering al-Qaeda. About two years later, the United States led the invasion that toppled Iraq's dictatorship.

In this book, readers will learn how the United States became embroiled in the conflict between North Korea and South Korea as a result of the Cold War and the desire to keep the spread of communism at bay. Participating in The Korean War under the umbrella of the United Nations became the model for future conflicts that continue to this day.

▲ In April 1951 South Korean refugees walk across a bridge that spans the Han River at water level on the outskirts of Seoul, South Korea, in order to escape the oncoming communist offensive.

CHAPTER 1

Setting the Stage for the Korean War

The Korean War was a violent, three-year conflict between North and South Korea that began in June 1950. The war was the first international conflict that the United Nations (UN) became involved in. At the request of the UN, nations from around the world, including the United States, fought on the side of South Korea. Troops from China and the Union of Soviet Socialist Republics (USSR or Soviet Union) joined with North Korea.

▼ *Korea is a peninsula in East Asia. It borders China and Russia in the north. Japan is located across the sea in the southeast. This map illustrates the division between North Korea and South Korea.*

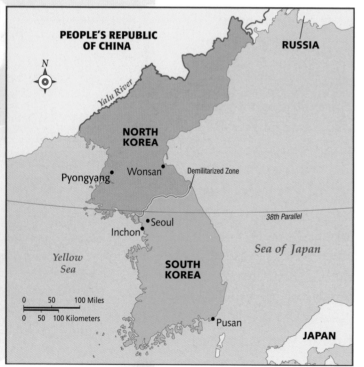

Dividing a Country

During World War II, the United States joined with the Allies, a group of nations that included Great Britain and the Soviet Union, to defeat the Axis powers (Germany, Italy, and Japan). The alliance was not always easy. U.S. politicians distrusted Soviet leader Joseph Stalin and his **communist** government. U.S. leaders watched as Stalin took control of large chunks of Eastern Europe after World

War II ended, consolidating his power and spreading communism throughout much of the area that had been under the control of Axis powers.

When Japan, the last Axis power, surrendered in August 1945, it was forced to give up Korea, which had been under Japanese control since 1910. In early September, U.S. troops landed in southern Korea to accept the surrender of the Japanese there, while Soviet troops accepted the surrender of the Japanese in northern Korea. In keeping with Stalin's plan to extend his influence and communism, the Soviet Union immediately began to seal off the section of the country that was north of the **thirty-eighth parallel**, a line of latitude that roughly divides Korea in half. The United States took control of the section south of the line.

Historians today continue to argue about why the Allies divided the country. Some say that the United States allowed the division because it did not want the Soviets to control all of Korea. Others say that the separation allowed the speedy removal of the Japanese in the country. Whatever the reasons, the division of the country between two superpowers with very different ideas about freedom and government would soon cause problems that would devastate the country and people of Korea.

The two areas soon created systems of government that were very different from each other. In the southern section, political parties quickly formed. All were dedicated to immediate independence. One party even proclaimed the south as the People's Republic of Korea. The U.S. military government, however, refused to recognize the new republic. The United States hoped to set up one government that would eventually govern a united Korea. In the meantime, the Koreans in the south were given an assembly, or

Korea is a land in East Asia. Throughout its history, the country has been attacked and conquered by its neighbors, including China, Mongolia, and Japan. For most of the period from 936 to 1910, however, Korea managed to remain an independent kingdom, governed by a series of kings and powerful families.

In 1905, Korea was invaded by Japan. Five years later, the country was **annexed** by Japan. Life under Japanese rule was harsh. During the first decade of control, Japan established a military government. Koreans who spoke out against the invaders were imprisoned or executed.

In September 1940, Japan entered World War II on the side of the Axis powers, Germany and Italy. During the war, Japan again imposed a military government on Korea. Hundreds of thousands of Koreans were forced to fight in Japan's army and work in its factories.

lawmaking body, that was elected, in part, by the citizens.

In the north, the Soviets set up a government that gave communist Koreans positions of power. One of the leaders was Kim Il-sung, a Korean who had lived in exile in China most of his life. During World War II, Kim headed a Korean battalion for the Soviets' Red Army. Now Kim helped create a northern Korean government patterned after the Soviet government.

▲ *Korean leader Kim Il-sung in Pyongyang, North Korea, in May 1979.*

The United Nations

Near the end of World War II, representatives from fifty countries had gathered in San Francisco, California, to create an organization that would work for global peace and promote human rights around the world. At the meeting, the countries drew up a **charter** establishing the United Nations. The new organization became official in October 1945, when twenty-six countries agreed to the charter. These countries included the United States, Great Britain, the Soviet Union, and China.

The problems in Korea quickly put the new organization to its first serious test. In May 1946, talks between the United States and the Soviet Union about how to go about reunifying Korea came to a halt with no solution. A year later, new talks between the two countries also stalled.

The Undeclared War

The Korean War was a war that was never declared by the U.S. Congress. Instead, Congress gave the president permission to send troops to Korea to protect democracy. Some people call the war a **police action**, with the United States and other countries acting as the police. These people prefer to call the war the Korean Conflict as a way of recognizing that war was never officially declared.

The conflict was one of the bloodiest in history, resulting in the death or injury of hundreds of thousands of troops. The war devastated Korea, resulting in the deaths of as many as three million people. Some died while fighting, but many more died from disease, starvation, and **exposure**. The United States played a key role, providing the most troops and supplies to South Korea during the struggle. Almost half a million U.S. soldiers fought in Korea during the war, and fifty-four thousand sacrificed their lives.

The Korean War is sometimes called the "forgotten war" because it was sandwiched between World War II (1939–1945) and the Vietnam War (1964–1975). While those two wars had overwhelming effects for most Americans at home, the Korean War had little immediate effect on the majority of U.S. **civilians**. Historians since the 1970s have tended to focus more on the Vietnam War than on the Korean War.

▼ *Troops of the Twenty-fifth U.S. Army Division are pinned down by enemy fire along the Hantan River in South Korea in April 1951.*

The Korean War, however, was an important conflict. It was the first major episode in the **Cold War** and had devastating, long-lasting consequences that continue to affect Koreans even today. It also set the precedent for the United States to become involved in undeclared wars and police actions in other countries, especially in defense of a democratic form of government.

CHAPTER 2

The Cold War

▼ *The western side of the Berlin Wall is guarded by French military police (on the left) and West Berlin customs officials. Behind the concrete wall, East Berliners work on an underground cable. The Berlin Wall became a symbol of the Cold War.*

Although the United States and the Soviet Union had fought on the same side in World War II to defeat the Axis powers, the relationship quickly fell apart once the war was over. During World War II, the Allies had agreed to allow countries that were occupied by Germany to hold democratic elections. As the Soviets drove German troops out of Eastern European countries, however, they installed communist governments. At the end of the war, Stalin refused to give up control of these countries.

The United States and other democratic nations watched in alarm as Stalin's communist empire grew larger, more powerful—and more dangerous. Before World War II, Stalin had used an iron fist to bring the Soviet Union under his control. During the Great Purge of the 1930s, he had imprisoned or executed anyone who opposed him. Now, world leaders watched as Stalin used the same tactics in Eastern Europe. From 1922 through 1953, the Soviet dictator would be responsible for the deaths of tens of millions of people.

After seizing control of the Eastern European nations, the Soviets isolated these satellite countries from any contact with the United States and other democratic countries. They censored communication and made trade difficult between communist and noncommunist nations. These barriers became known as the **Iron Curtain.**

Before long, the Cold War between the Soviet Union and the United States came to involve most of the world. The Soviet Union and the communist Eastern European nations that were controlled by Stalin were called the **Eastern bloc.** Opposed to them was the **Western bloc,** which included the United States, Western Europe, and other countries that believed the world should be made up of independent, democratic nations. Although no actual war between the United States and the Soviet Union was ever declared, both countries competed to have the strongest economy, the biggest military, and the most powerful weapons. In the years after World War II, the rivalry would bring the two superpowers to the brink of war several times.

The Truman Doctrine

As communism spread across Eastern Europe, the United States took action. In March 1947, U.S. president Harry S. Truman issued a statement that came to be known as the Truman **Doctrine.** The Truman Doctrine stated that the United States would come to the aid of any free nations fighting "attempted subjugation by armed minorities or by outside pressure." This meant that the United States would provide military support to any nation fighting a communist takeover. Although the statement was aimed at

Fast Fact

The term *iron curtain* was first used in 1819 to describe an impenetrable barrier. It came into popular use in 1946, after Winston Churchill, prime minister of the United Kingdom during World War II, used it in a speech to describe the Soviet sphere of influence and control of Eastern Europe.

The Marshall Plan

One way that the United States supported democratic nations in Western Europe was to send billions of dollars to help these war-torn countries rebuild. Under the European Recovery Plan, developed by Secretary of State George Marshall and commonly known as the Marshall Plan, the United States sent $13 billion in food and money to seventeen nations throughout Europe. The photo above shows a celebration marking the arrival of the *John H. Quick,* a ship that carried 8,800 tons (7,982 metric tons) of wheat to France in May 1948. This aid allowed the countries to feed their citizens, rebuild roads, factories, and farms, and strengthen their democratic governments. As a result, the Marshall Plan is thought to have prevented some countries from converting to communism. In 1953, Marshall was awarded the Nobel Peace Prize for helping Europe after the war.

communist rebellions in Greece and Turkey, it would set the tone for future U.S. involvement in Korea.

At this time, the United States was concerned with maintaining a balance of power between communist and noncommunist nations. Truman, like other politicians, believed that if one country established a communist government, then neighboring countries would as well. This belief later came to be known as the **domino theory,** because of the domino-like effect one country could have in pushing other countries to communism. The Truman Doctrine became the foundation of U.S. foreign policy aimed at actively preventing the spread of communism. This policy was known as **containment.** In 1949, the United States banded together with like-minded countries to found the North Atlantic Treaty Organization (NATO), a military coalition aimed at defending one another from communist attacks.

Korea Splits Apart

As concern about the spread of communism grew, the United States turned its attention back to the problem of a divided Korea. U.S. and Soviet politicians met throughout early 1947, but were unable to agree on a plan to unite the two sections of the country. In September 1947, the United States brought the issue of Korea's status before the United Nations.

The UN decided that national elections should be held throughout Korea. The UN hoped that Korea would be reunited under one government, chosen by the people. To make sure that the election was fair and legal, UN representatives offered to go to Korea and oversee the voting. The United States agreed with the UN. The Soviet Union, however, did not want the communists to lose control of North Korea. Communists in the northern part of Korea

The Korean War

refused to allow the UN to observe elections there. They also refused to recognize the results of any elections held in the south.

On May 10, 1948, people in South Korea elected a national assembly. This newly elected assembly then created the Republic of Korea (ROK), also called South Korea. The city of Seoul was chosen as the capital. The nation's first president was Syngman Rhee. From 1912 to 1945, Rhee had lived in the United States, trying to gather support for Korean freedom from Japan.

Rhee quickly showed himself to be a dictator who would not tolerate any opposition to his rule. He dissolved the country's assembly and outlawed political parties that opposed his policies. He even ordered the executions of some Koreans who spoke out against him. In this environment of repression, many people began to support communist rebel groups within the country.

▼ South Korean President Syngman Rhee talks with U.S. general Mark W. Clark, who became commander of the UN forces in Korea after Matthew Ridgeway. Clark would eventually sign the cease fire agreement with North Korea in 1953.

On September 9, 1948, the communist government in the northern section of Korea established the Democratic People's Republic of Korea, also known as North Korea. Pyongyang was chosen as the nation's capital, with Kim Il-sung as the first premier. Like Rhee, Kim was in complete control of his country's government. North Korea's "Great Leader," as Kim Il-sung was called, would remain firmly in charge of the nation until his death in 1994.

In October 1948, the Soviet Union proclaimed that North Korea was the only legal government in Korea. In December, the UN declared South Korea to

▲ The rise to power of Mao Zedong (pictured on posters), the leader of China, is celebrated in the streets of China by supporters of the communist revolution.

be the only legal government in the country. The border between the two new countries continued to be the thirty-eighth parallel. Despite two separate and very different governments, both nations claimed that they controlled all of Korea. Troops from the north and south often battled at the border.

In June 1949, most U.S. troops evacuated South Korea. About five hundred remained behind to help train the country's army. With most U.S. troops gone, South Korea became more vulnerable to communist attacks from the north and **guerrilla attacks** from within. South Korean soldiers also launched attacks against the north.

Atomic Bombs, China, and the "Red Scare"

On August 29, 1949, the Soviet Union tested its first atomic bomb. The event greatly alarmed the United States. Until this time, only the United States had possessed the knowledge of how to make atomic weapons. The test marked the start of an arms race between the United States and the Soviet Union. In the coming years, each nation would try to amass more—and more powerful—weapons to use in case of war.

Then, on October 1, 1949, Chinese communists toppled China's existing Nationalist government and took control of the country. The Nationalists had taken power in China in 1928, uniting the country under a one-party dictatorship. The communists, under Mao Zedong, renamed the nation the People's Republic of China. When news of the change

The Korean War

reached the United States, politicians became even more worried. Unlike the small Eastern European countries that had already fallen to communism, China was an important power in Asia that could influence smaller Asian countries to choose communist governments.

The recent events increased fear of communism in the United States. Many Americans feared the damage that could be done by communists within the country, although few Americans supported communism and fewer still were working to harm the country. The late 1940s, however, became known as the time of the "Red Scare" because some politicians started a campaign to root out dangerous communists in the United States. In February 1950, Joseph McCarthy, a U.S. senator from Wisconsin, falsely announced that he had a list of fifty-seven "known communists" who were working within the U.S. government. McCarthy was essentially accusing these people of being

▼ *During testimony in 1954, U.S. senator Joseph McCarthy of Wisconsin points to a map labeled "Communist Party Organization U.S.A. —Feb. 9, 1950."*

Soviet spies—that is, traitors who were disloyal to the United States. Although the so-called threat that these individuals posed to the United States was suspect at best, newspapers publicized the senator's claims, and in the atmosphere of suspicion and fear, many people believed McCarthy's charges. McCarthy, however, had only just begun. In the coming years, his accusations would ruin the lives and careers of many Americans.

▼ *This map illustrates the major advances of the participants in the Korean War, which began in 1950.*

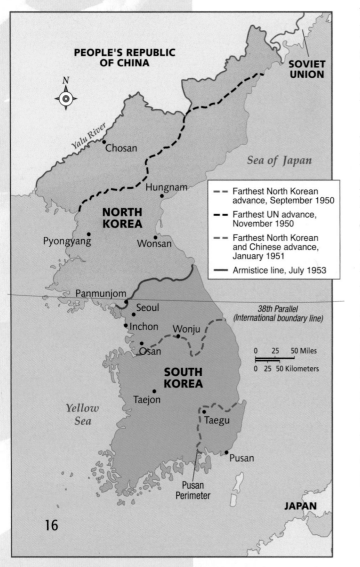

PEOPLE'S REPUBLIC
OF CHINA

SOVIET
UNION

N

Yalu River

Chosan

Sea of Japan

Hungnam

NORTH
KOREA

-- Farthest North Korean advance, September 1950
— Farthest UN advance, November 1950
-- Farthest North Korean and Chinese advance, January 1951
— Armistice line, July 1953

Pyongyang   Wonsan

Panmunjom

Seoul   38th Parallel
(International boundary line)

Inchon   Wonju

Osan   0   25   50 Miles
0   25   50 Kilometers

SOUTH
KOREA

Taejon

Yellow
Sea   Taegu

Pusan

Pusan
Perimeter   JAPAN

16

After the Japanese surrendered Korea in 1945, a civil war between north and south had begun. Although North Korea and South Korea had formed their own governments in 1948, neither side was willing to accept that Korea was no longer one nation. Fighting between the north and south only intensified after U.S. and Soviet troops left the region in 1949.

At daybreak on June 25, 1950, thousands of soldiers from North Korea crossed the thirty-eighth parallel and invaded South Korea. Their goal was to take control of South Korea and reunite the country under communist rule. They had 135,000 troops and plenty of airplanes, guns, and tanks. Many of these weapons were supplied to North Korea by the Soviet Union. The South Koreans, with only 95,000 soldiers, were outmanned and outgunned. The South Koreans were quickly overpowered and could only watch as the North Koreans marched toward Seoul.

Plea for Help

The UN believed that the aggressive attack by North Korea threatened world peace by bringing Cold War tensions between communist and democratic nations to a violent boiling point. The UN secretary-general, Norwegian Trygve Lie, said, "The invasion is assuming the character of full-scale war and may endanger the maintenance of international peace and security." At the request of the United States, the UN quickly passed a resolution demanding that North Korea remove its troops from South Korea.

▲ *South Korean refugees, many carrying all their possessions in wagons or on their backs, head south hoping to avoid North Korean troops in August 1950.*

North Korea refused to budge. Instead, North Korean troops continued to advance upon South Korea's capital. By June 27, they were outside Seoul. South Korean officials, including President Syngman Rhee, fled to Taejon, a city in southeastern South Korea. That day, the UN passed a resolution asking member nations to contribute weapons, troops, and supplies to aid South Korea.

As one of the five permanent members of the organization's important Security Council, the Soviet Union could have vetoed the entire resolution. At the time, however, the Soviet Union was boycotting the international organization because it refused to recognize China's new communist government.

The United States Gets Involved

Even before the UN voted to assist South Korea, President Truman had taken action. On June 27, the day before North Korea captured Seoul, Truman ordered the deployment of U.S. air and naval forces to aid South Korea. Three days later, he also ordered in ground troops. The first ground troops left the

United States on July 17, 1950. The twenty-five hundred soldiers were members of the army's Second **Infantry** Division. The troops, stationed in Fort Lewis, Washington, set sail from Tacoma.

Over the course of the Korean War, the United States would supply about 90 percent of all foreign troops, equipment, and supplies used in the battle between North and South Korea. In all, about 480,000 U.S. soldiers fought in Korea. They supplemented the 590,000 South Koreans who would sign up over the coming three years to defend their country.

U.S. Reaction

On July 19, President Truman addressed the nation for the first time about the Korean War. Truman's speech was broadcast by radio across the nation. At this time, television was just developing as an important form of communication and entertainment. In 1950, radio was still the primary means of spreading important news.

Most Americans supported Truman's decision to send U.S. troops to aid South Korea in battling communist aggression. The president told the country that communists in Korea and elsewhere were working to bring an end to democracy and free government around the world—and that they must be stopped.

U.S. citizens also supported the war because they believed that it would be a short one. Most remembered—and wanted to avoid—the number of deaths of U.S. soldiers that resulted from the United States' four-year involvement in World War II. Troop commanders, also believing that the war would end quickly, announced that U.S. troops would be home by Christmas 1950.

The United States did not formally declare war on North Korea. This made it possible for Truman to bypass Congress and take immediate action.

Congress, however, supported his decision to send troops to South Korea.

As the conflict dragged on, however, opponents of the war began speaking out—in Congress and elsewhere—against Truman. Some began calling the Korean War a police action that was costing the United States lives and money. When asked by a reporter if the conflict in Korea was a police action, Truman agreed. He told the reporter that the United States was helping the UN "repel a bunch of bandits." The term *police action* eventually became the official language of the government. Some historians think that Truman wanted to avoid causing the public discomfort by using the term *war* to describe the conflict.

Other Nations Help Out

U.S. politicians strongly believed that the democratic nations of the world must present a united front in the face of communist aggression in Korea: North Korea's actions threatened international peace, and all nations must take part to end the threat.

Most of the member nations of the UN pledged to help South Korea in any way that they could. During the course of the war, fifteen countries supplied more than thirty-six thousand troops to fight alongside U.S. soldiers. Five more countries sent teams of medical workers to support the combat troops. Many other countries contributed by sending equipment, food, medical supplies, and other aid.

Although the number of troops from other nations was small compared to the number of U.S. soldiers fighting in Korea, their presence was important. The United States needed to show the Soviet Union and other communist countries that free nations around the world stood together, united, against the spread of communism.

Fast Fact

In addition to the United States, fifteen countries sent combat troops to Korea: Australia, Belgium, Canada, Colombia, Ethiopia, France, Great Britain, Greece, Luxembourg, Netherlands, New Zealand, Philippines, South Africa, Thailand, and Turkey. Five nations sent groups of medical workers: Denmark, India, Italy, Norway, and Sweden.

CHAPTER 4

The Struggle Begins

On July 1, four days after North Korea took Seoul, three divisions of U.S. soldiers landed at Pusan, the southern tip of South Korea. They had been stationed in Japan, so they were able to arrive before other troops from the United States. The soldiers quickly moved into battle positions about 75 miles (121 km) south of Seoul.

The first battle between Allied and North Korean troops took place on July 5, 1950, at Osan, 30 miles (48 km) south of Seoul. (The Allied forces, at this point, consisted of troops from the Eighth U.S. Army Division, U.S Air Force, and Republic of Korea forces.) The U.S. regiments numbered 406 men, while North Korea had more than 4,000 troops. There was no way that the United States could defeat such a large group. Instead, its goal was to delay the North Koreans from advancing further south before the arrival of more U.S. troops.

As the communists attacked, U.S. soldiers quickly learned that their ammunition was no match for the big Soviet tanks that the North Koreans used. The U.S. soldiers, however, were able to hold the North Koreans off for

▼ U.S. soldiers make their way from the train station at Taejon, South Korea, to the battlefront in July 1950.

seven hours before running out of ammunition. U.S. forces then retreated. About 120 U.S. soldiers were killed during this first battle of the war, and thirty-six were taken prisoner. Most of the prisoners later died in North Korean prison camps.

General MacArthur Takes Charge

On July 8, General Douglas MacArthur, a seasoned military commander, was given command of UN forces in Korea. This meant that MacArthur was in control of all U.S. (Army, Navy, and Air Force), South Korean, and international troops, collectively called the Allied Forces. The general chose Tokyo, Japan, as his headquarters. Lieutenant General Walton H. Walker commanded the ground forces in Korea.

Throughout July and into early August, MacArthur's troops unsuccessfully battled the communist soldiers, trying to regain Seoul. During a one-week period in mid-July, nearly 30 percent of all U.S. troops in Korea were killed or wounded. North Korean troops continued to advance south, reaching the Pusan Perimeter by August 1950. The Pusan Perimeter was a battle line in the southeastern corner of Korea that roughly followed the Naktong River. Once the communists took control of the territory south of the Pusan Perimeter, there would be little left for the Allied troops to do but surrender.

The North Koreans, however, had been weakened during their advance. As they marched south, they had lost thousands of men as well as weapons and other supplies. On the Allied side, new units of troops and better weapons continued to arrive in southeast Korea. By early August, Allied troops outnumbered the North Koreans.

On August 5, the battle for the Pusan Perimeter began. The North Koreans crossed the Naktong

General Douglas MacArthur

Douglas MacArthur, pictured above, devoted nearly his entire life to the U.S. military. The son of an army officer, MacArthur grew up on army posts in New Mexico. He later wrote that his first memory was the sound of an army bugle. He graduated from the U.S. Military Academy at West Point, then served as an aide to President Theodore Roosevelt. During World War I, MacArthur served in France.

Many of MacArthur's military commands were in the Far East. He served in the Philippines for many years, as well as in Japan. In 1944, he was made a five-star general, the highest possible rank in the U.S. Army. One of MacArthur's finest moments came on September 2, 1945, when he accepted the Japanese surrender that ended World War II. After the war, he was named Supreme Commander of Allied Powers in Japan.

River, but they did not get very far. Three weeks later, after heavy fighting, Allied troops forced them back across the river. In early September, fighting still continued along the Pusan Perimeter. The battles here were among the most deadly of the war, resulting in the deaths of more than thirty-six hundred U.S. soldiers. Many more were wounded. The theater of war, however, was about to shift northwest to a port city in South Korea called Inchon.

The Second Campaign

While his troops battled it out along the Pusan Perimeter, MacArthur came to realize that he needed another plan to drive the North Koreans out of Seoul. Late in the evening of September 15, he led U.S. soldiers and marines in an **amphibious assault** on Inchon, a city 25 miles (40 km) southwest of the South Korean capital. During the attack, only a few marines were wounded, and none were killed. The assault was successful, and Inchon, formerly under communist control, was now firmly back in the hands of the Allies. The thirteen thousand U.S. troops stationed around Inchon cut off North Korean troops along the Pusan Perimeter, isolating them from other North Korean troops north of the city.

With the success of the Inchon landing, the course of the war changed. Allied troops began the march to Seoul to retake South Korea's capital. On September 25, U.S. soldiers and marines entered the capital. The following day, General MacArthur announced that Allied troops had recaptured the city.

Back at the Pusan Perimeter, Allied troops fought their way past North Korean troops and joined the rest of the UN forces in Seoul. It seemed that the war had been won. The North Koreans had been driven back across the thirty-eighth parallel, and Syngman Rhee was returned to power. Military leaders now gathered to decide on their next move. Had they won? Or was there more to be done? President Rhee certainly thought so. He wanted the Allied forces to defeat the communists in North Korea and reunite the country with him as its ruler. U.S. military leaders had other motives for wanting to advance into North Korea. First, they hoped to destroy the communist military and prevent the north from ever invading South Korea again. Second, by capturing part of North Korea, U.S. forces hoped to set up a buffer zone between Allied troops in South Korea and communist China.

▲ A U.S. Marine helicopter picks up personnel from a landing barge in the harbor at Inchon in September 1950. U.S. troops hoped to capture the port city in their drive toward Seoul.

Into North Korea

After retaking Seoul, MacArthur was given permission by the UN to invade North Korea. The communist army had been severely reduced during the past months of fighting, and the conquest of North Korea seemed an easy task. In early October, South Korean troops crossed the border between the two countries and captured the cities of Wonsan, Hungnam, and Hamhung. On October 19, Allied forces captured Pyongyang, North Korea's capital. The Allied troops pursued the communist soldiers as they fled north, toward China's border with Korea. On the way, the Allied soldiers found the bodies of sixty-six American prisoners of war and civilians. North Korean soldiers had executed the prisoners and then the civilians as they had fled north.

China was alarmed. It did not want Allied troops threatening its border. China sent a message warning the Allies to halt and turn around. General MacArthur, however, wanted a quick end to the war. He also believed that, with the conflict nearly at an end, China would not become involved. He ordered his troops to continue forward.

China Steps In

On October 25, China entered the war on the side of North Korea. On that day, Chinese soldiers attacked and nearly wiped out a regiment of South Korean soldiers north of Unsan in the North Hamgyong region. As more reinforcements, including UN forces, U.S. Army troops, and ROK soldiers, arrived, the Chinese held their ground. Fighting here continued for nearly two weeks before the Chinese retreated to the mountains.

The United States hoped that China had decided to withdraw from the war. Unaware of the strength and technical skill of the Chinese army, Truman thought the Chinese were only threatening to enter the war to force the United Nations to ask the United States and the Allied Forces to withdraw from the Korean **peninsula**. With the Chinese gone, U.S. soldiers still believed that they could end the war by Christmas. On November 25, however, as UN forces pressed north, China launched the second part of its attack against Allied troops.

The number of Chinese troops was overwhelming, and the damage to the Allied troops was immense. The week from November 26 through December 2 was the bloodiest, most deadly week for the United States in the war. In all, more than thirty-five hundred men were killed, and many more were wounded. The worst day of fighting was November 30. On that day alone, nearly eight hundred U.S. soldiers lost their lives.

▼ A photograph sent by the China Photo Service in communist China to a picture agency in New York in September 1950 was described as "a group of young volunteers for the Korean People's Army marching to a recruiting station." The picture of young Chinese men was intended to illustrate China's interest in Korea, although it is unclear whether the recruits were really volunteering to serve or had been coerced by their government.

The Korean War

On December 4, Allied troops began evacuating Pyongyang. In the coming days, U.S., UN, and South Korean troops retreated to the port of Hungnam. From here, 105,000 troops and 17,500 military vehicles were transported by ship to South Korea. The military also transported 98,000 Korean refugees, fleeing from North Korea. Had there been room and time, thousands more would also have left. The last ship left Hungnam on Christmas Eve.

During the course of the war, China would send 780,000 troops to aid North Korea's military. The Soviet Union also threw its support behind North Korea. The Soviets sent about 25,000 military personnel (pilots and other advisers), in addition to equipment, including guns, ammunition, and tanks.

Anticommunist Hysteria

Back in the United States, people were astounded that China had become involved in the war and attacked American troops. President Truman was also surprised. He had believed MacArthur's assurances that China would stay out of the conflict. On December 16, 1950, Truman declared a national emergency. Under a state of emergency, certain federal laws could be disregarded, while other emergency measures were put in place. For example, the process for ordering military equipment was made simpler and the law requiring an eight-hour workday was temporarily suspended for defense-related industries. This meant that the military could more easily order weapons and that factories could more quickly manufacture them. It also meant that workers in these factories could now be required to work longer hours.

Truman further increased the anxiety and fear felt by many Americans when he implied that the United States might use nuclear weapons against China.

▲ *Students at Public School 152 in Queens, New York, act out a scene from the 1951 Federal Civil Defense film called* Duck and Cover, *designed to teach youngsters what to do in the event of a raid by a foreign enemy or a possible nuclear showdown between the Cold War powers.*

Such an attack on a communist nation, it was feared, might encourage the Soviets to use their own nuclear weapons against the United States or U.S. targets elsewhere in the world.

U.S. citizens now entered an era when worrying about a nuclear attack became normal. In schools, children were taught to "duck and cover," taking shelter beneath their desks. Some people built or purchased bomb shelters, underground bunkers that they hoped would protect them from the effects of nuclear radiation. This atmosphere of fear would continue until the early 1980s, as the two superpowers engaged in an arms race to amass the most nuclear weapons.

McCarthyism

The entry of China into the Korean War also gave new energy to Senator McCarthy. In the summer of 1950, an investigation conducted by the U.S. Senate had found McCarthy's charges that communists worked for the U.S. government to be false. After the retreat of UN forces in December 1950, however, Americans were more worried than ever by the threat of communism. Seizing his chance, McCarthy continued his attack on ordinary citizens who he claimed were spies for the Soviets or disloyal to the United States. McCarthy was accusing people of treason with little credible evidence. In many cases, he knew that the accusations were untrue. He thus destroyed the lives and careers of innocent people. In the coming years, "McCarthyism," the practice of accusing people of being communists, became widespread across the nation.

The Korean War

McCarthy used information about suspected communists that was given to him by J. Edgar Hoover, the head of the Federal Bureau of Investigation. He even targeted President Truman and some members of his cabinet, accusing them of being "soft" on communism. Truman could do little to counter McCarthy. Few politicians dared to oppose the Republican senator.

In 1953, McCarthy was made head of the Senate Permanent Subcommittee on Investigations. The job of the subcommittee was to investigate communists in government agencies. Over the next year and a half, McCarthy's committee called more than 650 people to testify privately about their—or their friends' and coworkers'—involvement with communism. Those who refused to cooperate were then made to testify publicly in televised hearings.

It was not until 1954 that someone dared to defy McCarthy. After the Korean War, McCarthy held televised hearings in an attempt to show that U.S. Army officers had also been soft on communists. By now many people were fed up with McCarthy's tactics. On June 9, Joseph Welch, a lawyer for the U.S. Army, attacked the senator head-on. After McCarthy accused a young colleague of Welch's of belonging to a private lawyers' club that McCarthy suspected of having communist leanings, Welch exploded. "Until this moment, Senator, I think I never really gauged your cruelty or your recklessness," he told McCarthy. "Have you no sense of decency, sir, at long last? Have you left no sense of decency?"

Many historians believe that Welch's outburst against McCarthy's brutal tactics was the beginning of the end for the senator from Wisconsin. Later the same year, McCarthy was censured, or officially reprimanded, by the U.S. Senate for his conduct. He died less than three years later.

The House Un-American Activities Committee

In 1938, the House of Representatives set up a special investigating committee, known as the House Un-American Activities Committee (HUAC). During World War II, HUAC investigated people living in the United States who were accused of being sympathetic to the Nazi government in Germany. After the war, communism became the committee's next target. Federal and state officials, scientists, and other workers around the nation were forced to swear oaths of loyalty to the United States. Even people in Hollywood—directors, writers, and actors—were not safe. Those thought to be communists were **blacklisted**. Others were asked to give the names of coworkers known to have communist sympathies.

During the Korean War, members of HUAC traveled throughout the country, searching out communists in colleges, state governments, and labor unions in major U.S. cities. After the war, HUAC began to lose its power and importance. In 1975 it was abolished by the House of Representatives.

CHAPTER 5

An End in Sight?

The Chinese were encouraged by their easy victory over Allied troops in North Korea. At the end of December, communist leader Mao Zedong approved plans to push U.S. troops out of South Korea also and reunite Korea under one communist government. On January 4, 1951, Chinese and North Korean soldiers once again captured Seoul.

Ridgway Arrives

Allied troops were not ready to give up. They now had a new commander, Lieutenant General Matthew B. Ridgway. Ridgway had replaced General Walton Walker in December 1950, after Walker was killed in a car crash during the retreat from North Korea.

The army's new commander was a dynamic leader. After the retreat from the north, he had stepped in and soon boosted the spirits of the demoralized Allied troops. Always prepared for battle, Ridgway constantly wore a hand grenade strapped to his shoulder.

In many ways, Ridgway's career had been

▼ General Douglas MacArthur (far right) is accompanied by some of his officers, including Lieutenant General Matthew B. Ridgway (far left), as he surveys the front line near Suwon, Korea, in 1951.

similar to MacArthur's. He, too, had graduated from the U.S. Military Academy at West Point. He had served in the Far East, including China and the Philippines, and he had led successful missions during World War II.

Under Ridgway's command, the soldiers rallied. Over the next two months, the Allies forced the communist troops further and further north. U.S. planes bombed enemy supply lines, depriving the North Koreans and Chinese troops of badly needed food.

On March 14, 1951, Allied forces once again drove communist forces out of Seoul. By the end of the month, the Allies had pushed the enemy back over the thirty-eighth parallel.

The Fall of a Hero

Since the retreat from North Korea, President Truman had been unhappy with the way MacArthur was conducting the Korean War. MacArthur favored expanding the war into China, while Truman preferred to keep the war limited to Korea.

On March 24, MacArthur, without Truman's permission, issued a public statement to the Chinese. He offered to meet communist officials in China to discuss diplomatic options, at the same time threatening an invasion if the Chinese did not comply. On April 11, Truman fired General MacArthur as commander of Allied forces in Korea, replacing him with Ridgway. As a final insult to the general, MacArthur heard about his dismissal over the radio before being officially notified.

The Battle of the Hills

By June, Allied troops and communist troops were at a standoff. After months of bloody, bitter fighting,

A Warm Welcome

In April 1951, the people of the United States were shocked to learn that General Douglas MacArthur had been fired by President Truman. MacArthur was already a legendary figure in U.S. history, and many people were outraged at his abrupt dismissal. One such person was Senator Joseph McCarthy, who called for Truman's impeachment. McCarthy even suggested that the president had been drunk when he fired the war hero. The U.S. Senate launched an investigation into Truman's actions. At the end of the investigations, the Senate quietly supported the president's decision by refusing to issue any report on the firing.

When MacArthur returned from Korea, it was the first time he had been back in the United States since World War II. He was given a hero's welcome, complete with parades and public appearances. The Republican Party even tried to convince the former general to run for president. Instead, MacArthur chose to live out the rest of his life quietly in New York City. He died in 1964.

both sides had dug in just north of the thirty-eighth parallel. China's army had failed to retake Seoul.

On June 23, the Soviet representative to the UN proposed that UN and communist leaders from North Korea and China sit down together for peace talks. On July 10, General Ridgway, North Korea's Kim Il-sung, and Chinese military leader Peng Dehuai met at Kaesong, a city just a few miles northwest of Seoul that was now occupied by the communists, to conduct peace talks. The discussions did not last long. The two sides could not agree to an agenda for the meetings, let alone a peace agreement. By August 22, the talks had been suspended.

As the peace talks ground to a halt, the temporary truce also fell apart. Fighting—some of the most bitter and bloody of the entire war—began again. The Allied troops fought to advance into North Korea, and the communists fought just as fiercely to hold them back.

This part of the war became known as the Battle for the Hills because the Allied troops fought to capture hills, bridges, and other targets located along the thirty-eighth parallel. Although military officials identified the hills by numbers—Hill 346, Hill 717—soldiers on the ground came up with other, more colorful names—Heartbreak Ridge, Pork Chop Hill, Old Baldy, and Bloody Ridge. Throughout the rest of the war, bloody battles for these small pieces of ground would result in the deaths of hundreds of U.S. soldiers.

▼ U.S. troops carry wounded soldiers to an aid station just behind the front lines in South Korea in October 1951. The two-week battle at Heartbreak Ridge on the east central front of Korea saw some of the war's fiercest fighting.

The Korean War

On October 25, Allied and communist officials once again met to discuss bringing the war to an end. This time, the talks were held in Panmunjom, a village in central Korea. These peace talks would continue, on and off, for nearly two years.

Documenting a War

The Korean War was documented from beginning to end by military photographers and cameramen. These specialized soldiers went along with the troops into battle and on missions. They photographed and filmed the action as it was happening. Between September 1951 and December 1952, they sent home more than 1 million feet (305,000 meters) of motion picture film as well as sixty-one thousand photographs. Much of this historic footage can now be found in the National Archives in Washington, D.C.

Reporters from U.S. newspapers were also allowed to accompany troops into battle in Korea. As a result, the public had more firsthand, eyewitness information available about this war than about any previous one. At first, the reporters were expected to use their own judgment when reporting news from Korea. After some stories criticizing the United States and its allies appeared in American and British papers, however, news reports after December 1950 were censored by the U.S. military. One story with a negative slant, published in a British magazine, described South Korea's mistreatment of communist prisoners. It included photographs.

Although the number of televisions in American homes continued to grow in the early 1950s, this new medium did not greatly affect how people learned about the war. Korea would be the last war during which U.S. citizens relied on newspaper accounts and radio broadcasts to get their information.

Marguerite Higgins

Reporter Marguerite Higgins was told by U.S. Army officers that Korea during wartime was no place for a woman. Her own newspaper, the *New York Herald-Tribune,* even ordered her to come home, but the feisty California native refused. Instead, she remained in Korea, dodging bullets with soldiers on the front and reporting the news from the battlefield. Higgins was no stranger to wartime reporting: During World War II, she had been the first reporter to cover the liberation of Dachau, a German concentration camp.

Higgins's hard work in Korea paid off. In 1951, she became the first female reporter to win the Pulitzer Prize for journalism. Higgins continued her wartime reporting in Vietnam. Her career was cut short when she died in 1966 of a tropical disease she caught while covering the war there.

CHAPTER 6

The War Drags On

In 1952, most soldiers in Korea saw few signs that the war would end soon. Even while the UN negotiated peace with North Korea and China, fighting between the two sides continued. Over the coming months, however, the line of battle would remain at the thirty-eighth parallel. At this time, more than 314,000 U.S. troops were stationed in Korea, making up 90 percent of all UN troops.

A Tour of Duty

In 1951, the U.S. Congress had extended **selective service**, more commonly called the draft, to increase the size of the military. The Korean War draft included all qualified men between the ages of eighteen and a half and twenty-six.

▲ A U.S. soldier, exhausted by battle duty, slumps down to rest alongside his machine gun dugout while Allied forces guard the Pusan Perimeter in August 1950.

Men who were drafted had to serve twenty-four months of active duty. This two-year period was known as a tour of duty. By the end of the war, more than half of all American soldiers in Korea had been drafted (rather than volunteered). About 1.5 million American men were drafted during the Korean War.

Arriving in Korea, the men were issued uniforms, which were much the same as those worn by soldiers during World War II. During Korea's cold, snowy winters, the men were issued boots, gloves, hats, and wool undergarments, pants, and sweaters to help them stay warm. In warmer weather, the woolen garments were replaced by cotton ones. The soldier's set of clothes was known as "general issue," or GI. As a result, American soldiers in Korea were called GIs.

In addition to clothing, the GI carried other supplies necessary to survival in the open. These items included a canteen, cup, spoon, sleeping bag, and poncho.

Feeding the fighting men in Korea was no easy task. A six-month supply of meat required 19,600 cattle, 71,000 hogs, 794,600 chickens, and 65,900 turkeys. Hundreds of acres of vegetables and fruit—including potatoes, cabbage, peas, corn, apples, and peaches—were grown by American farmers to feed the soldiers. Most of the fruits and vegetables were canned, but some were shipped fresh from ports on the West Coast in refrigerated ships. Because the water in Korea was of poor quality, most soldiers drank fruit juice shipped from the United States.

Most of the food, clothing, and other supplies used by U.S., South Korean, and other Allied soldiers came from the United States. These goods were sent from forty-nine military depots all around the nation to the ports of San Francisco and Seattle and from there sent on to Japan and Korea. Japan and Korea also supplied some of the food needed by Allied troops.

U.S. citizens back home contributed to the cause by donating blood to help wounded soldiers. The American Red Cross collected the blood, which was then shipped to a military blood-processing laboratory in California. From there, the blood was flown to Japan, to be used for American GIs as needed.

Reckless

For marines of the Fifth Regiment, a Korean horse named Reckless proved a bright spot during the war's darkest days. Reckless carried weapons and shells from the ammunition supply point to the guns at the front. Sometimes, when enemy fire was heavy, Reckless made the trip on her own. Descended from a famous South Korean racehorse, Reckless endeared herself to the marines by eating poker chips, hats, and Coca-Cola. In June 1957, the commander of the Fifth Marine Regiment made the brave horse a staff sergeant and awarded her a medal for bravery. She retired to Camp Pendleton, California.

▲ Thousands of U.S. Marines suffered frostbite during the Battle of Chosin Reservoir in North Korea in December 1950. In this photograph, two soldiers try to find a few moments of rest despite the freezing temperatures.

Life of a Soldier

The life of a soldier during a tour of duty usually consisted of long stretches of boredom followed by short periods of intense fighting. While waiting for combat, soldiers did their best to keep busy. They took photos, listened to music, played cards, and wrote letters to friends and loved ones back home. To combat boredom, the United Service Organization (USO) flew entertainers from the United States to Korea to perform for the troops. During the war, Bob Hope, Marilyn Monroe, and Groucho Marx were just a few of the entertainers who traveled to Asia to entertain U.S. troops.

Although most **casualties** of the war were hit by shell fragments from **mortars** and grenades, many soldiers suffered from noncombat injuries and disease in Korea. One serious problem was trench foot, a painful foot disease that for many soldiers resulted from spending many hours in cold, wet rice paddies. Other wintertime dangers were exposure and frostbite, which affected thousands of soldiers. Disease took a toll too. Korean War soldiers were plagued with colds, flu, hemorrhagic fever, hepatitis, and encephalitis.

Segregation and the Korean War

In World War II, African American soldiers had performed bravely in **segregated** divisions. This meant that blacks and whites served in separate units. In 1948, President Truman issued an order that all soldiers, regardless of their race, were to be

The Korean War

treated equally. Despite this order, most soldiers continued to serve in segregated units during the early years of the Korean War.

As the war progressed, however, African Americans were assigned to white units. With the success of these integrated units, the army became more willing to allow blacks and whites to fight side by side. By 1953, 95 percent of all fighting units were integrated. The last all-black unit was dissolved after the war, in 1954.

The decision to end segregation put the U.S. military far ahead of the rest of the nation in providing civil rights for African American citizens: Most of the United States remained segregated. Black veterans who had fought side by side with white soldiers during the war came home to find themselves the victims of racial discrimination in housing, employment, and throughout society. One black veteran was turned away from an all-white barbershop in California even though he was wearing his military uniform.

Women in the War

Women played an important role in the Korean War. At the outbreak of the war in 1950, about twenty-two thousand women were enlisted in the U.S. military. Although they were prohibited from taking part in combat, they performed many other necessary roles. Military women served as interpreters, stenographers, aides, and administrators at army hospitals. Others worked in mess halls, post offices, motor pools, and at army headquarters in Japan.

Hundreds of women worked as army nurses in Korean hospitals, in MASH units, and on hospital trains, treating wounded Allied and communist troops. Combat nurses started blood transfusions, gave shots, and treated many types of injuries, from battlefield wounds to frostbite. The nurses faced the

The First MASH Units

The Korean War marked the first use of the mobile army surgical hospital (MASH). These traveling medical units included operating rooms, beds for recovery, and all the medical equipment needed to help wounded soldiers survive the battlefield. MASH doctors and nurses were flown into battle zones by helicopter, allowing for quick, efficient treatment for those injured in battle. The MASH units worked so well that they were also used in the Vietnam War and the Persian Gulf in 1991. In the 1970s and early 1980s, a television show called *M*A*S*H* made the work of these medical units familiar to Americans across the country. The show, set in a MASH unit in Korea, combined drama and comedy to express the horror and absurdity of war.

A Military Code of Conduct

As a result of the experiences of Korean War POWs, the U.S. military created a code of conduct that was approved by President Dwight D. Eisenhower in 1955. The code set out rules for all U.S. soldiers to follow. It included the following:

I will never surrender of my own free will.

If I am captured I will continue to resist by all means available. I will make every effort to escape and aid others to escape.

When questioned, should I become a prisoner of war, I am bound to give only name, rank, service number and date of birth. I will evade answering further questions to the utmost of my ability.

I will never forget that I am an American fighting man, responsible for my actions, and dedicated to the principles which made my country free. I will trust in my God and in the United States of America.

same combat dangers as soldiers. They braved heavy gunfire and other armed assaults. A nursing shortage in the United States put combat nurses in high demand. Over the course of the war, as many as fifteen hundred women served in Korea as army nurses.

Prisoners of War

Besides the chance of being killed or wounded on the battlefield, soldiers faced still another danger in the combat zone—being captured by the enemy and held as a prisoner of war (POW). Allied POWs held by North Korea endured nightmarish conditions. Many U.S. soldiers were murdered soon after they were taken prisoner by communist troops. Those who survived the first days of captivity were often forced to march to temporary prison camps far behind enemy lines. Food, medicine, and shelter were all scarce at these camps. Many POWs died of disease, starvation, or exposure. In one camp, four out of every ten POWs died within three months. Later, Chinese military officials created permanent POW camps, where conditions were better.

North Korean and Chinese POWS fared better under Allied treatment. The Allies were able to supply adequate food and shelter. This was no small task, because at one point in the war, the Allied forces had more than eighty thousand North Korean and Chinese troops imprisoned. After the war, both sides accused the other of mistreating prisoners. For example, the UN forces were accused of massacring large numbers of communist POWs. The communists were accused of brainwashing, beating, and torturing Allied prisoners. The charges on both sides led the UN to pass a resolution that condemned all acts of torture and cruelty against prisoners of war.

CHAPTER 7

Ending the War

As talks between the two sides dragged on, one of the sticking points was the exchange of prisoners. China and North Korea insisted that *all* their POWs be returned, even those prisoners who did not want to go home. In March 1953, the UN reached a partial agreement with the communists to exchange sick and wounded prisoners. With that issue resolved, the peace talks at Panmunjom resumed. Sick and wounded prisoners were exchanged the following month.

▼ *The demilitarized zone (DMZ) and the tunnels running underneath it are illustrated on this map. The tunnels were first discovered by the United States in the mid-1970s and new tunnels were found as late as 1990, leading U.S. experts to believe that they run along the entire 2.5-mile (4-km) strip.*

Peace

On July 27, 1953, the UN, China, and North Korea signed a cease-fire agreement. South Korea, however, did not sign the document that led to an end to the fighting. In 1954, representatives of the United States, China, North Korea, South Korea, and other countries that had fought in the war met in Geneva, Switzerland, to hammer out a permanent peace treaty. The two sides were unable to come to any agreements. To this day, neither North Korea nor South Korea has signed a treaty to put a permanent end to hostilities.

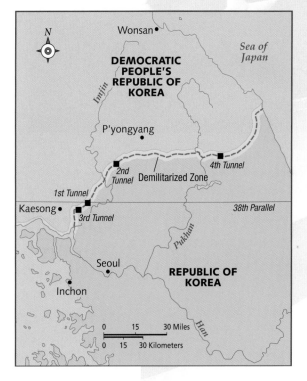

37

Under the terms of the cease-fire agreement, the **demilitarized zone** (DMZ) was established. This neutral strip of land stretched along the final line of battle, 2.5 miles (4 km) wide on either side. Both North Korea and South Korea agreed to keep their military forces at their present strength. The cease-fire also provided for a full exchange of POWs.

In August 1953, the prisoner exchange began. More than thirty-five hundred American POWs were released, but others remained unaccounted for. Throughout the war, U.S. troops had reported seeing the bodies of murdered Americans, executed by the communists. Now, the military feared the worst for those who had gone missing in action (MIA).

Some communist prisoners decided not to return home. More than twenty-two thousand Chinese and North Korean POWs refused to be **repatriated**. These former communists were allowed to stay in South Korea or Taiwan. Taiwan, an island off the southeast coast of China, was the seat of the deposed Nationalist government of China. During the war, the United States had sent troops to prevent the island from being attacked by Chinese communists.

▲ *Private First Class Thomas S. Farrell of Colorado disembarks from a North Korean truck at Panmunjom during the final phase of a prisoner exchange—called Operation Big Switch—between the Allies and the communists in August 1953.*

U.S. Troops Return Home

In October, U.S. soldiers began leaving South Korea. Because the war was not officially over, the U.S. military left behind equipment for South Korea, as well as some troops to help defend the nation in case of communist attack. Before the troops departed, the United States issued a stern warning to North Korea:

The Korean War

If the country continued to harass its southern neighbor, it faced the possibility of nuclear attacks.

Back home, the soldiers were not given the same sort of welcome that the veterans of World War I and World War II had received. Most were given little or no public celebration. It seemed that many U.S. citizens preferred to forget the undeclared war that had cost their country so much in so little time.

Catherine Neville, a nurse who served in both the Korean War and World War II, later recalled talking to a fellow war nurse about the reception of the Korean War veterans. "The saddest part of this...is nobody knows you've been away or where you've been," Neville told her friend. "You'll know that when you get home. Nobody will notice it." Another veteran, after being honored in South Korea in 2003, said, "When I got off the boat after the war, the Red Cross gave me a doughnut and a cup of coffee, and that was it. There was no publicity, no heroes' welcome. This is the first time I've been honored."

The Casualties of War

The Korean War was one of the deadliest conflicts in history. More than 560,000 UN and South Korean troops were killed, wounded, or reported missing. In addition, about one million South Korean civilians were killed during the war. An estimated 1.6 million communist troops were casualties of the war, along with an unknown number of North Korean civilians.

For the United States alone, the toll was devastating. More than fifty-four thousand U.S. soldiers died in Korea, and another one hundred thousand were wounded. More than five thousand were taken prisoner or declared missing in action.

After the war, relations between the United States and the communist powers continued to get worse.

Fast Fact

The Korean War is often called "The Forgotten War" because of the United States' neglect in honoring its veterans or remembering the conflict that cost so many American lives.

In the coming years, the United States and the Soviet Union would square off—unofficially—many times. For nearly four decades, the United States and the Soviet Union engaged in an arms race, with each side developing bigger and more powerful nuclear weapons. The standoff between the two nations would continue until the breakup of the Soviet Union in 1991.

Problems between the United States and China also continued. For many years, the United States refused to officially recognize the communist government there. In return, China steadfastly refused to have any diplomatic or economic relations with the United States. Over the past two decades, however, the two nations have become more friendly. The United States agreed to recognize the communist government in 1979. In 2000, President Bill Clinton granted China permanent normal trade relations and lifted sanctions against the country. Today, China is one of the United States' top trading partners.

The Korean War was the first war that the United States did not win. It changed how many Americans felt about getting involved in international disputes. After the war, public opinion polls in the United States revealed that nearly seven out of every ten Americans thought that the war had been too costly (the United States spent about $67 billion fighting the war and more than fifty-four thousand Americans lost their lives) and should never have been fought. Despite such public sentiment, the conflict was not the end of U.S. involvement in Asia. In 1965, the United States would send troops to protect South Vietnam from attacks by communist North Vietnamese troops. Again, thousands of U.S. soldiers would fight for democracy during an undeclared war in a divided country.

CHAPTER 8

The Forgotten War

Fifty years after the Korean War ended, more than eight thousand American servicemen remain unaccounted for in Korea. Most of them are thought to be dead—killed in action—but efforts to learn what happened to them continue. As late as 2005, families of the missing men and veterans' groups have traveled to South and North Korea to try to learn about U.S. soldiers who went missing during the war and to recover their remains. As a result of these trips, the possible remains of more than 180 Americans were returned to the United States. The exact fate of the rest of these soldiers in Korea remains unknown.

▼ *Some of the nineteen statues that make up the Korean War Veterans Memorial are lined up for placement at the memorial site in Washington, D.C. The statues, depicting men on patrol, include members of the U.S. Army, Navy, and Marine Corps.*

They Served in Korea

Here are just a few well-known people who served in Korea.

Roberto Clemente. After the war, Clemente went on to play baseball with the Pittsburgh Pirates.

Bill Cosby. The well-known comedian served in the U.S. Navy during the war.

Ed McMahon. McMahon, a TV personality, took part in eighty-five missions in Korea.

Ted Williams. The Boston Red Sox star also served in World War II.

In 1995, the Korean War Veterans Memorial in Washington, D.C., was officially dedicated to honor the men and women who served in Korea. The monument shows life-sized statues of Korean War soldiers, dressed in battle gear, on patrol. The site also includes a black granite wall showing the images of two thousand people who fought in the war, a United Nations Wall honoring the countries that supported South Korea, and a pool whose edge is carved with the words "Our nation honors her sons and daughters who answered the call to defend a country they never knew and a people they never met." Since 1995, millions of people have visited the memorial to **pay tribute** to those who served in Korea.

North and South Korea Today

Years after the end of UN involvement in the Korean conflict, tensions between North Korea and South Korea remain. In 1967, North Korean troops attacked South Korean soldiers in the DMZ. Sixteen years later, North Korean terrorists killed seventeen South Koreans who were on an official state visit to Burma (now Myanmar). In 1988, North Korea boycotted the Olympics because South Korea was hosting the games.

In 1991, hopes for a settlement between North Korea and South Korea arose when the prime ministers of the two countries agreed to once again begin working on a permanent peace treaty. Nothing came of that agreement, however, and the two leaders did not meet. Finally, in 2000, the leaders of both countries met together for the first time since 1948. Family members in the two countries, cut off from each other since the beginning of the war, were allowed to visit. Transportation routes and economic ties between the two countries were also repaired—on a limited basis.

Despite some progress, U.S. troops still remain in South Korea to discourage North Korean aggression. In 1968, North Korean troops seized a U.S. spy ship, the *Pueblo*. To avoid another war in Asia, President Lyndon Johnson quietly negotiated the safe return of the *Pueblo*'s crew members. In 1976, two U.S. military officers were beaten to death by a group of North Korean soldiers in the DMZ. Days later, North Korea's leader issued a statement that called the deaths only "regrettable."

In 2002, North Korea alarmed international politicians by revealing that it was developing nuclear weapons. It also withdrew from the Nuclear Nonproliferation Treaty (NPT), an agreement it had signed in 1985. The NPT, created in 1968, stated that those nations with nuclear capabilities would not give information on how to build nuclear weapons to any other country. The nations without nuclear weapons that signed the treaty promised to refrain from building nuclear weapons. In early 2005, North Korea informed the world that it had, in fact, built a nuclear weapon. Seven months later, North Korea agreed to stop building these weapons and allow UN inspectors into the country in exchange for international aid. The very next day, however, the North Korean government went back on its word, stating that it would not halt its nuclear program unless the United States provided nuclear equipment for producing electricity. Today, while South Korea and the United States continue to be allies and trading partners, North Korea remains an unpredictable international hot spot. Whether or not its claims of nuclear capability are true or false, it is certain that North Korea is working hard on its program and refusing to come to a diplomatic compromise with the United States and the rest of the world.

Kim Dae-jung

One man who is committed to creating peaceful relations between the two Koreas is Kim Dae-jung, pictured above *(right)*, a South Korean politician. Kim began his political career by speaking out against the military dictators who controlled South Korea from 1961 to 1987. As a result, he spent many years in prison or under house arrest. In 1982, he was even forced to leave his country for ten years.

In 1998, Kim was elected president of South Korea, a post he held until 2003. Throughout his time in office, Kim worked to smooth relations with North Korea. In 2000, he traveled to Pyongyang to join his North Korean counterpart, Kim Jong-il, pictured above *(left)*, in a historic meeting. Kim Dae-jung was awarded the Nobel Peace Prize in 2000 for his efforts to reconcile the two Koreas, countries that share the same history but are still worlds apart.

TIME LINE

1945	World War II ends and Japan surrenders Korea.
	The United Nations is founded.
1947	The UN decides that a country-wide election will determine what form of government Korea will have.
1948	The people of South Korea establish the Republic of Korea.
	Communists in North Korea set up the Democratic People's Republic of Korea.
1949	U.S. troops evacuate South Korea.
	The Soviet Union detonates its first atomic bomb.
	Communists take control of the Chinese government.
1950	North Korean troops invade South Korea and take Seoul.
	The first U.S. and UN troops arrive in Korea.
	The battle for the Pusan Perimeter begins.
	MacArthur and his troops capture Seoul.
	Allied forces capture Pyongyang.
	China enters the war on the side of the North Koreans.
	Allied forces begin a retreat from North Korea.
	President Truman declares a national emergency.
1951	Chinese and North Korean troops retake Seoul.
	Allied forces recapture Seoul and force communist troops back to the thirty-eighth parallel.
	Truman fires MacArthur.
	Peace talks begin but last little more than a month.
	Peace talks resume.
1953	Both sides agree to exchange sick and wounded prisoners.
	UN, North Korean, and Chinese officials sign a cease-fire agreement.
	The communists and Allied forces exchange all prisoners of war.
	U.S. soldiers begin leaving South Korea.

GLOSSARY

amphibious assault a coordinated attack that includes forces on sea, on land, and in the air

annexed joined or added

blacklisted suspected of being a communist and prevented from being hired

casualties soldiers who are wounded, captured, or killed during a war

charter a document that spells out an organization's goals and laws

civilians people who are not in the military

Cold War a period of rivalry and tension between communist nations like the Soviet Union and noncommunist nations like the United States, beginning after World War II and lasting until the 1980s

communist describing a system of government in which property is owned by the state and shared by all citizens

containment U.S. foreign policy developed after World War II that focused on stopping the spread of communism

demilitarized zone (DMZ) the neutral strip of land separating North and South Korea

doctrine a statement of government policy, especially in international relations

domino theory the belief that the acceptance of communism by one country would directly cause its acceptance by others

Eastern bloc the Soviet Union and other communist countries in Eastern Europe

exposure the condition of being out in the open and unable to take shelter from sun, rain, snow, or other severe weather

guerrilla attacks ambushes by civilian fighters

infantry soldiers who are trained to battle on foot

Iron Curtain trade and communication barriers imposed by the Soviet Union between communist and noncommunist nations

mortars weapons that fire shells into the air

pay tribute to show gratitude and respect

peninsula a piece of land almost entirely surrounded by water

police action a localized military action undertaken without a formal declaration of war

repatriated sent back to one's own country

segregated separated by race or some other characteristic

selective service the practice of choosing citizens between certain ages to serve in the military

thirty-eighth parallel a line of latitude that cuts through Asia, Europe, and North America

Western bloc democratic nations, including the United States and most of Western Europe

About the Author

Robin Doak is a writer of fiction and nonfiction books for children, ranging from elementary to high school levels. Subjects she has written on include the human body, profiles of U.S. presidents, athletes, and American immigration. Robin is a former editor of *Weekly Reader* and, in addition to her extensive experience writing for children, has also written numerous support guides for educators. Robin holds a Bachelor of Arts degree in English, with an emphasis on journalism, from the University of Connecticut.